Behind The Terror

The War on Terrorism

By John Hamilton

Visit us at
www.abdopub.com

Published by ABDO & Daughters, an imprint of ABDO Publishing Company, 4940 Viking Drive, Suite 622, Edina, Minnesota 55435. Copyright ©2002 by Abdo Consulting Group, Inc. International copyrights reserved in all countries. No part of this book may be reproduced in any form without written permission from the publisher.

Printed in the United States.

Edited by Paul Joseph
Graphic Design: John Hamilton
Cover Design: Mighty Media
Photos: National Archives, AP/Wide World, Corbis, U.S. Air Force

Library of Congress Cataloging-in-Publication Data

Hamilton, John 1959-
    Behind the terror / John Hamilton.
        p. cm. — (War on terrorism)
    Includes index.
    Summary: A survey of terrorism, its history, and how it relates to religion and world politics today.
        ISBN 1-57765-659-8
    1. Terrorism—Juvenile literature. [1. Terrorism—Miscellanea. 2. Questions and answers.]
I. Title. II. Series.

    HV6431.H345 2002
    363.3'2—dc21

                                                    2001056667

Table of Contents

The Unthinkable Happens

A woman watches in horror as the World Trade Center burns and then collapses.

Searching For Answers

WHY DO THEY HATE US? THAT'S THE question Americans asked themselves in the wake of the terrorist attacks of September 11, 2001. It seemed impossible that fellow human beings could use airliners as missiles and launch them into American cities, wiping out scores of people as easily and unthinkingly as someone might stomp on an anthill.

After the attacks, shocked Americans groped for answers. Who are the terrorists? What do they want? Why do they hate us so much that they're willing—even eager—to kill innocent people by the thousands?

The answers to these questions are many and complex. Trying to understand terrorism is not easy—experts can't even agree on how to define it. But as citizens of a free democracy, Americans have a duty to learn, and to see behind the terror. Only by understanding the terrorists can people hope to root them out and destroy their networks.

Terror on the Battlefield

A *scene from Pieter Brueghel the Elder's* The Triumph of Death.

Terrorism And War

**M**ANY PEOPLE BELIEVE TERRORISM IS A recent trend, but it has a long, bloody history. Terrorism has been around for thousands of years, used by armies and other armed groups to gain power by striking fear into the hearts of innocent citizens.

Throughout history, most armies have used terror in one way or another to weaken their opponents. The ancient Romans, during the Third Punic War against the Carthaginians in 149 B.C., employed terror tactics against the enemy capital of Carthage. Nine of every ten civilians in the city died from disease, starvation, or Roman raids. After the war, the survivors were sold as slaves, and the remains of their city were destroyed.

When the Huns and other barbarians from Asia swept through Europe in the fourth century A.D., they killed many people in their path. It made no difference to them whether the victims were soldiers or civilians; they were all enemies to the Huns.

Eight hundred years later, the Mongol hoards slaughtered anyone who resisted them, sometimes wiping out entire cities. When they sacked Baghdad (in present-day Iraq) in 1258, tens of thousands of innocent people were slain.

Even in twentieth-century wars, the armies of the world have intentionally targeted civilians. World War II was especially brutal in this way. Strategic bombing was a new military idea that used heavy, long-range aircraft to pulverize cities. The hope was that enemy civilians would become so demoralized and sick of war that they would pressure their governments to surrender. (World War I saw some aerial bombing of cities, but nothing compared to the scale of terror inflicted on civilians in World War II.)

In 1940, after the successful German invasion of France, Adolf Hitler ordered his air force to bomb cities in Great Britain—especially London—in an attempt to batter the English people into submission. (In reality, strategic bombing of civilian targets had just the opposite effect. People, especially in England, Germany, and Japan, emerged from the bombing campaigns even more resolved to hold out against the enemy.)

The Allied powers also resorted to terrorizing civilians in World War II. American and British planes dropped thousands of tons of bombs over German cities, killing countless civilians. On March 9, 1945, American B-29 aircraft dropped incendiary bombs on Tokyo, Japan, setting the city ablaze and killing nearly 100,000 people. Later that summer, the U.S. dropped atomic bombs on the Japanese cites of Hiroshima and Nagasaki, killing more than 120,000 men, women, and children. In World War II, for the first time in history, more civilians than soldiers were killed.

The U.S. defended the use of nuclear weapons in Japan by pointing out that their use greatly shortened the war, and made an invasion of Japan by Allied forces unnecessary. Hundreds, if not thousands, of American lives were probably saved. Still, the world was sickened by the slaughter of innocent civilians in Japan, England, Germany, and elsewhere. This reaction against terror bombing forced a drastic cutback in its use in future wars.

Today's armed forces, especially the United States, rely more and more on guided bombs and missiles that seek out military targets. The U.S. has developed a huge arsenal of precision-guided weapons, sometimes called "smart bombs," that avoid civilian casualties as much as possible.

Today most armed forces claim they don't intentionally target civilians. Unfortunately, another threat has surfaced: the use of innocent bystanders as pawns in political struggles and revolution. It is the new face of terror.

Targeting Civilians

The ruins of Nuremberg, Germany, after the Allied bombing raids of WWII.

Terrorist or Freedom Fighter?

A leader of FLN, Algeria's armed militant group, in French custody in 1960.

Anti-Colonialism

TERRORISM TODAY IS MOST OFTEN THOUGHT of as groups of people, unhappy with their current government or economic situation, that kill innocent civilians to draw attention to their cause. But there is no clear definition of terrorism. People disagree on just what it means. One person's terrorist is another person's freedom fighter.

Nelson Mandela, the former president of South Africa, committed terrorist acts while fighting the minority white rule of apartheid. Today, many consider him an honored statesman. Two former prime ministers of Israel, Menachem Begin and Yitzhak Shamir, used terrorism while struggling to create an independent Jewish state free from British rule in the late 1940s. These groups struck at military targets and symbols of the government, but innocent people were also killed.

After World War I, Great Britain was handed control of Palestine by the League of Nations. Armed conflicts between Jews and Arabs became frequent. Shortly after World War II, Menachem Begin became the leader of Irgun, an extreme nationalist Jewish group that endorsed violence when necessary. It was also violently anti-Arab.

Irgun was a militant Zionist group. Zionism is a movement that began in the late nineteenth century because of growing anti-Semitism. This hatred of people who practiced Judaism reached a horrifying peak during the German Holocaust of World War II. Millions of Jews were put to death. To escape religious persecution, Zionists wanted to re-establish a Jewish homeland in Palestine, where the Israelites once ruled in ancient times.

In order to carve out a Jewish state in Palestine, Irgun guerrillas committed terrorist acts and assassinations against British occupation forces and Palestinian Arabs. In July 1946, the group bombed Jerusalem's King David Hotel. The hotel was a headquarters for the British, and therefore a legitimate military target, according to Irgun. But 91 people died, including Jews and Arabs, as well as Britons.

Political struggle is a key element in today's definition of terrorism. If a raving lunatic uses a machine gun and kills a dozen people in an office building, that is not terrorism. The motive of the terrorist is political, a grab for power. It is also premeditated and carefully planned.

Terrorism is a tool that weak groups use to fight overwhelmingly powerful governments. It is an act of desperation. Terrorism uses or threatens violence with the hope of far-reaching psychological damage beyond the initial attack. It is the deliberate creation of fear in order to change a government or its policies. Through fear, and the publicity that fear generates, terrorists create power.

At the beginning of the twentieth century, many countries were colonies, controlled by the world's superpowers. The British, French, Dutch, and American empires stretched to every corner of the globe. Later, the Soviet Union built its own communist empire to counter the threat from the Western powers.

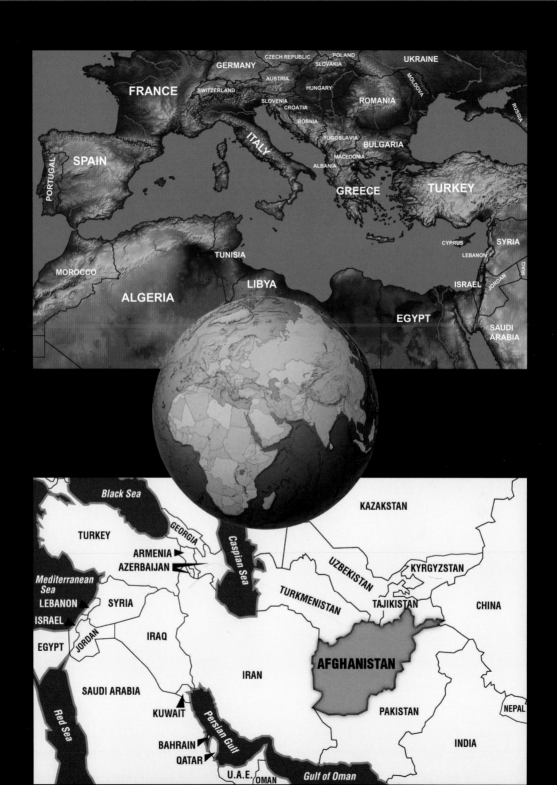

Terror in Palestine

The King David Hotel in Jerusalem, Palestine, after being partially destroyed by a bomb blast July 22, 1946.

Starting in earnest at the end of World War II in 1945, many countries pushed for independence. These countries did not want to return to pre-war colonial status—they wanted to govern themselves. Naturally, the superpowers were reluctant to let their colonies go free. In many cases, though, independence finally won out, sometimes peacefully. But all too often, armed resistance sprang up.

In the late 1940s, armed Jewish militants struck targets in Palestine relentlessly until the British public could not stand any more. Irgun's attack on the King David Hotel was particularly brutal. The British public was sickened by the violence. World opinion, especially that of the United States, forced the British to act. In 1948, Britain formally ended its occupation of Palestine, and the country of Israel was soon born. (Menachem Begin, branded a terrorist by the British, would go on to become prime minister of Israel, even winning the Nobel Peace Prize in 1978, together with Egyptian President Anwar Sadat.) Using the Jewish revolt as a model, anti-colonial groups soon sprang up all over the world, most notably in Cyprus and Algeria.

In post-war Algeria, in northern Africa, the French were slow to grant freedom, which earlier had been promised. To gain world attention to their struggle, Muslim terrorist groups waged a revolt that lasted from 1954 to 1962. At first, the terrorists targeted French military offices and buildings, without directly attacking people. When the French cracked down, however, and started executing revolutionaries, the terror campaign took an even bloodier turn. In 1956, the Algerians unleashed a wave of bombings, assassinations, and terror that deliberately targeted French civilians, including children.

Anti-Muslim rioting gripped the country. The rioting was followed by another wave of assassinations by the terrorists. The French army was finally called out to restore order. In their zeal to crush the terrorists, however, the army resorted to torture and other brutal measures, even against people merely suspected of being associated with the revolutionaries. The native Algerian Muslim community was outraged by this overreaction. Popular support for the terrorists swelled.

The excesses of the French military also outraged the public back home in France. South Africa's Nelson Mandela was once given advice by an Algerian revolutionary that "international opinion... is sometimes worth more than a fleet of jet fighters." The French army had dealt the Algerian terrorist organization a severe blow, but at the cost of political defeat. The brutal terrorism was too high a price to pay for the people of France. Within five years, the French withdrew from Algeria. After 120 years of French occupation, Algeria was finally granted its independence.

It's important to understand the history of anti-colonial terrorism in order to understand how terrorism has evolved into the terrible problem that it is today. The Jewish Irgun, the Cypriots, and the Algerians were able to attract international sympathy and support for their regional struggle. Attracting attention is key to the terrorists' cause.

Oppressed people everywhere saw how international pressure helped the terrorists get what they wanted. New groups soon sprang up and began applying this powerful lesson in places such as Northern Ireland, Quebec, Spain, Indochina, parts of Latin America, Germany, and Italy, as well as the Middle East. By the late 1960s, however, terrorism transformed, becoming a problem that would concern every country in the world.

Algerian Uprising

An Algerian soldier working for the French military guards a group of captured FLN soldiers.

Palestinian Rage

A masked terrorist armed with an AK-47 automatic weapon during an anti-Israeli rally.

International Terrorism

THE FIRST ARAB-ISRAELI WAR WAS FOUGHT IN 1948 and 1949. After the British left the region and Israel declared independence on May 14, 1948, several neighboring Arab countries attacked Israel. They objected to the Jewish state, considering the land Israel occupied to be Arab territory.

Arab armies from Egypt, Syria, Jordan, Lebanon, and Iraq invaded Israel. But even though the Jewish military forces were small, through superior tactics and fighting skill they were able to beat back the Arabs.

During the war, hundreds of thousands of Palestinian Arabs left or were forced from their homes, fleeing to the safety of neighboring countries. No one knows exactly how many Palestinians were forced out, but between 400,000 and 950,000 people were soon settled into refugee camps in Jordan, Syria, Lebanon, and Egypt.

The Palestinian refugees hoped that the Arab countries would regroup and crush Israel, so they could return to their homes. But the Arab countries were unprepared to launch another war so soon. To this day, thousands of Palestinians are trapped in the poverty of squalid refugee camps. Their status today is a big factor in the Arab-Israeli conflict.

By the mid-1950s, groups of desperate Palestinians realized that if they were ever to reclaim their homeland, they would have to do it themselves. Armed terrorists soon began attacking targets inside Israel. These attacks contributed to a second war between Israel and its Arab neighbors called the Six Day War.

The war was a resounding victory for the Israelis, who took control of the Gaza Strip, the West Bank, and the Golan Heights. Even with all of this fighting, few outside the region cared about the plight of the Palestinians. In 1968, however, Palestinian terrorists took their struggle outside the Middle East, and soon the whole world took notice.

On July 22, 1968, three Palestinian terrorists hijacked an Israeli El Al jet bound from Rome to Tel Aviv, Israel, and diverted it to Algeria. They demanded that Palestinian prisoners in Israel go free, or else they threatened to kill the plane's passengers. After 40 tense days of negotiations, both the passengers and hijackers finally went free.

Although nobody was killed during the hijacking, it marked the beginning of what we consider to be modern terrorism. Armed militants were now traveling outside their home bases and targeting civilians who had nothing to do with the terrorists' cause. Terrorism had become international, with the intention of shocking the world. The media storm that resulted brought the militants exactly what they wanted: attention.

Plane hijackings, which became more violent and bloody over the next several years, shed light on the Palestinians' cause. Dr. George Habash, founder of the group that carried out the 1968 hijacking, said, "When we hijack a plane it has more effect than if we killed a hundred Israelis in battle... For decades world opinion has been neither for nor against the Palestinians. It simply ignored us. At least the world is talking about us now."

Media Attention

In Amman, Jordan, terrorists blow up one of three hijacked airplanes on September 12, 1970, after removing their hostages.

In 1972, the world was shocked at the level of violence inflicted by international terrorism. It was a watershed year in which appalling violence, fear, and media frenzy all came together.

The summer Olympic Games that year were held in Munich, West Germany. On September 5, Arab terrorists from the Palestine Liberation Organization (PLO) stormed into the apartments of the Israeli Olympic team. They immediately killed two athletes and took nine others hostage. The terrorists demanded the release of fellow militants held in Israeli jails.

The Munich attack was a way for the PLO to attract media attention to their cause by attacking something of great value, a country's star athletes. It worked. More than 500 million people around the world watched on television as the hostage drama unfolded.

After 20 hours of tense negotiations failed, the terrorists attempted to leave the country with the hostages. German police tried to free the athletes in a shoot-out at the Munich airport, but the attempt went disastrously wrong. In the end, 11 Israelis, five terrorists, and one German police officer were dead.

Even though the terrorists failed to free their fellow militants in Israel, the PLO considered the operation a spectacular publicity success: it focused world attention on the Palestinian people and their plight. The era of terrorism as a live television event had begun.

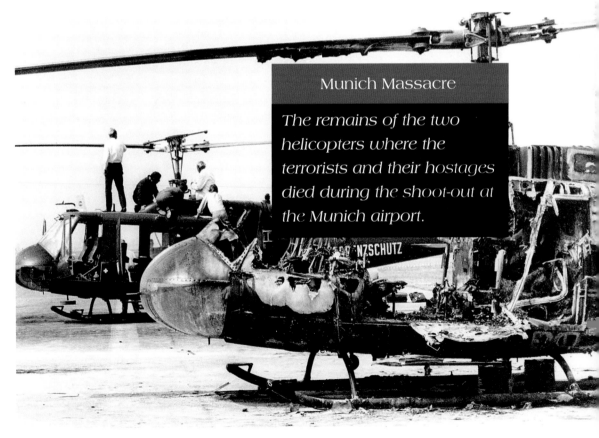

Munich Massacre

The remains of the two helicopters where the terrorists and their hostages died during the shoot-out at the Munich airport.

Hatred Fueled by Religion

A terrorist supporter holds the Koran, the Muslim holy book, during the funeral procession of a slain militant.

Religious Terrorism

ALL OF THE TERRORIST GROUPS AND movements discussed so far have been dominated by political goals. One of the most important emerging motives for terrorism today, however, is religion. The revolution that gripped Iran in 1979, transforming it into a hard-line Islamic republic, has played a crucial role in this transformation of modern terrorism. However, religious terrorism is not limited to the Middle East, or to Islam. Religious terrorists have emerged all over the world.

Yigal Amir, the young Jewish extremist who murdered Israeli Prime Minister Yitzhak Rabin in 1995, told police he committed the crime in order to stop the Middle East peace process. "I acted alone," said Amir, "and on orders from God."

This same belief has fueled the violence inflicted on innocent civilians, especially in the last 10 years. Islamic HAMAS suicide bombers continue to blow themselves up on crowded Israeli buses and street corners. Japanese followers of the Aum Shinrikyo cult in 1995 unleashed nerve gas in the Tokyo subway system, killing 12 and injuring thousands.

The American Christian Patriot movement stresses a paranoid anti-government belief, fueled by religion. It produced the likes of Timothy McVeigh, who bombed the Alfred P. Murrah Federal Building in Oklahoma City, Oklahoma, killing 167 men, women, and children.

Religion and terrorism have gone hand in hand for centuries. Two thousand years ago the Jewish Zealot movement fought against the Romans with a ruthless series of assassinations. They cut their enemies' throats with daggers, often in crowded marketplaces in plain sight of the public.

The Thuggees of central India (from whom we get the word *thug*) committed murder to serve Kali, the Hindu goddess of terror and destruction. Unsuspecting travelers were ritually strangled. The Thuggees killed as many as one million people until the British colonial police crushed the movement between 1831 and 1837.

The Assassins were a radical Muslim cult who practiced terrorism between 1090 and 1272. They fought to drive out Christian crusaders through ritual murder, with the Assassins often getting killed in the process. This self-sacrifice for religion, or martyrdom, is often seen in modern terrorism.

When we think of religious terrorists today, what often springs to mind are Islamic militants based in the Middle East, especially suicide bombers who kill innocent civilians in the name of God. The roots of this radical movement can be traced to the Iranian Revolution.

In 1979, Islamic fundamentalists ousted the Shah of Iran, their ruler, who was supported by the United States. A revolutionary government controlled by Islamic clerics replaced the monarchy. They made laws based on a very strict interpretation of the Koran (the holy book of Islam). The most powerful of these clerics was

Ayatollah Ruhollah Khomeini, who urged his followers to spread their faith. "We must strive to export our Revolution throughout the world," he said.

To spread Islamic law, the use of violence was officially permitted. It was justified on the grounds of self-defense from Western influence. The problems of the region were seen as coming from the West, especially the United States. Iranian clerics preached *jihad* (holy war) against the forces of the Great Satan, which is how they branded the U.S.

On November 4, 1979, armed militants stormed the American embassy in the Iranian capital of Tehran. They held approximately 70 Americans captive in an ordeal that lasted 444 days. It was a humiliation to the U.S. that helped bring about the downfall of President Jimmy Carter.

Many Muslims, especially terrorists and their recruits, see the Iranian Revolution as proof that the fundamental teachings of the Koran can be used to push back Western influence. A shift in the goals of terrorism took place as radical Islamic law spread. Instead of merely seeking attention for a political cause, the new terrorism sought to wipe out the other side. The former leader of Lebanon's Hezbollah terrorist group said, before Israeli commandos killed him in 1992, "We are not fighting so that the enemy recognizes us and offers us something. We are fighting to wipe out the enemy."

Terror networks based in the Middle East sprang up as an offshoot of the clerical Islamic state in Iran. Countries such as Iraq, Syria, Taliban-controlled Afghanistan, and Sudan, as well as Iran, actively supported these groups. This is what is meant by state-sponsored terrorism. These international terror networks get support from their host countries in order to function, buy weapons, and recruit new members.

For most of the 1980s, the Soviet Union fought a losing war in Afghanistan. It had invaded the country in 1979 in order to keep Afghanistan's Communist government in power. But the Soviet army could not defeat the fanatical international brotherhood of *mujahideen*, who fought a guerrilla war for Afghanistan's freedom. After suffering tremendous casualties over a 10-year period, the Soviets finally withdrew from the country. Afghanistan soon fell into the hands of the Taliban, a government based on an ultra-strict interpretation of the Koran.

"Holy Warriors"

A Muslim mujahideen fighter prays beside a tank in the mountainous region of Tora Bora, Afghanistan.

Islamic militants, including Saudi Arabian millionaire and terror organizer Osama bin Laden, saw the victory of the *mujahideen* over the Soviets in Afghanistan as proof of the supremacy of faithful Muslims over the weak infidel powers. They believed that the superior armed forces of a superpower were no match for the zealots' superior will.

Some people think Islam is an intolerant and violent religion. Most scholars disagree. Islam is one of the world's major religions, with more than one billion followers. It began more than 1,400 years ago, and has had a great impact throughout history in literature, the arts, science, and medicine. Islam prohibits suicide, and condemns the murder of innocent people.

Many Muslims (followers of Islam) are frustrated by the lack of understanding of their religion in the West. As'ad AbuKhalil, a professor of political science at California State University, Stanislaus, said, "Don't judge us by our kooks. Western people need to remind themselves that religious Muslims are very similar to religious Jews and Christians. They believe in basic things like prayer—not hijacking and terrorism." AbuKhalil says that Islamic terrorists, especially Osama bin Laden and his al-Qaeda network, are distorting Islam for their own political purposes.

The most populous Muslim country in the world is Indonesia, with 170 million followers. Pakistan and Bangladesh are next, with 243 million followers combined. India and Turkey, both democracies, have 165 million Muslims. Only when you reach the Middle East do you find the most rabid anti-Western, anti-American feelings, backed by radical Islamic fundamentalism. Obviously something happened in the region to spark these feelings, something beyond religion. But what?

Anniversary of Hate

A U.S. flag is burned during a demonstration in Tehran, Iran, marking the anniversary of the seizure of the U.S. embassy.

Anti-Americanism

ARAB RAGE AGAINST AMERICA IS THE result of a combination of events that have happened in the Middle East over the past half-century. Most Muslims in the world, the peaceable majority, do not harbor the ill will that marks the terrorist organizations. The vast majority wants peace. But there is enough of a radical minority to form a formidable terrorist threat.

The hatred this radical minority carries with it is fueled by history. Militant Muslims resent the West for pushing back the march of Islam into Europe centuries ago. They remain bitter over the Crusades of the Middle Ages, in which Christian armies invaded the Middle East and killed millions of Muslims. And they are still angry at the years of colonialism the region endured during the past century.

The militants' goal today is to push Western influence out of the Islamic realm, to stamp it out completely and regain the glory of the past. They still believe in the supremacy of Islam. The forces of anti-Western hostility want to reverse history, and they want their extreme form of Islam to dominate the world.

Fueling Arab hatred today, first and foremost, is U.S. support for Israel, which receives nearly $4 billion in aid each year. The U.S. also sells advanced weapon systems to the Israelis. Many Arabs see Israel as an alien nation that doesn't belong in the region, and that oppresses Arab rights. They are especially angry that Israel has control over Islamic shrines in the city of Jerusalem.

Israel is a functioning democracy in the region, but it is seen as a puppet of the West. The extremists want nothing less than for Israel to be wiped off the face of the Earth.

Another reason Islamic militants hate the West is the desperation and poverty of the people of the Middle East. The rulers of the region's countries have a long history of collecting vast wealth and failing to use it to help their people. Despite huge sums of money from selling oil to the Western world, the people of the region get little benefit. In Egypt alone, the unemployment rate is 25 percent.

The economies of the region are stagnant, and many of their governments are brutal regimes that think nothing of killing anyone who disagrees or makes trouble. The common people of the Middle East see the United States supporting many of these countries in order to guarantee a steady supply of oil. They feel that the United States doesn't care about the plight of the common Arab; it only cares about its own interests, leaving the Arabs to wallow in their poverty and misery.

There are no real political parties in the Arab world, and there is no free press. The common people have no voice, and they feel powerless to change their situation. Radical Islam grew because it gave people a sense of meaning and purpose, a clear guidepost on how to live their lives. The mosques, Muslim houses of worship, became places where politics could be discussed, and actions could be planned against the oppressors.

Mideast Poverty

Residents of this Cairo, Egypt, neighborhood live in the shadow of a cement factory. In 1996, Cairo had the highest levels of lead and other pollutants in the world.

Terror Mastermind

Osama bin Laden, leader of the al-Qaeda terrorist network and prime suspect behind the September 11 attacks on America.

Osama bin Laden

RADICAL MUSLIMS CALL THE UNITED STATES the Great Satan because it is the most powerful country in the Western world. These radicals hate the Western democratic values, and they want to stamp out anything American in the region.

During the Persian Gulf War of 1990 and 1991, U.S. troops were based in Saudi Arabia to keep Iraq from invading. If the Saudi oil fields had been taken over or destroyed by Iraq, it would have been a major disaster for the U.S. economy. After the war, the Saudi royal family invited U.S. forces to stay in order to protect the country from future invasion.

To Muslim extremists, the United States is an evil force that is directly opposed to Islam. One such extremist is Saudi millionaire Osama bin Laden. He and other radical Muslims were outraged that the unbelievers, the infidels, were now trampling on holy ground. Saudi Arabia is home to two of Islam's most holy shrines in the cities of Mecca and Medina. The very thought of U.S. troops occupying his homeland enraged bin Laden and his terrorist followers.

In 1998, bin Laden called for a holy war, a *jihad*, against the United States. He issued a *fatwa*, a religious ruling, that called for Muslims to kill Americans, including civilians. Bin Laden wants the U.S. out of the Middle East because "For over seven years, the United States has been occupying the lands of Islam in the holiest of places... plundering its riches, dictating to its rulers, humiliating its people..." But bin Laden won't settle for merely ejecting the U.S. from the Middle East. He wants nothing less than the Great Satan's total destruction.

Bin Laden and his terrorists hate the West. Their religious goal is to drive Western values from the holy ground of Islam. And the main engine of Western values is the United States. Since they don't yet have access to weapons of mass destruction, the terrorists' goal is to first humiliate the U.S., just as the hostage crisis during the Iranian Revolution humiliated the superpower. The attack of September 11, 2001, was aimed not only to terrorize Americans, but also to humiliate the U.S., by attacking the symbols of the U.S. military (the Pentagon) and economy (the World Trade Center). Earlier attacks on U.S. embassies in Africa in 1998, and the USS *Cole* in 2000, were also meant to strike America symbolically. They were a warm-up for the terror to come.

The al-Qaeda network aims to attack the U.S. again and again, until the superpower is brought to its knees. The reward for the terrorists, according to *their* beliefs, is an eternity of comforts in heaven. This is a very tempting message for millions of young men stuck in the squalor and poverty of Middle Eastern countries. They are without hope, without future, and they're angry.

The terrorists have the will and fanaticism to destroy the U.S. If they ever get their hands on weapons of mass destruction, such as nuclear bombs or germ warfare agents, there is little doubt they will try to use them.

Pentagon Aftermath

Photographers document the clearing of the rubble in the damaged section of the Pentagon September 15, 2001, in Washington, D.C.

Terror Menace

A masked Fatah militant holds his gun during a rally at the Jebaliya refugee camp north of the Gaza Strip, January 1, 2002.

What To Do About Terrorism?

NOTHING JUSTIFIES TERRORISM. KILLING innocent people just to make a political statement is a barbaric act that must never be tolerated. Terrorism must be fought whenever it appears. This moral clarity helped to defeat the Nazis and fascists of World War II, and it can help to defeat the terrorists of today.

Terrorism can be fought in several different ways. First of all, people must not simply conclude that terrorists are insane. And it's not true that just poverty breeds terrorists. Instead, people must realize that terrorists are the products of failed societies that breed anger and resentment. Many experts agree that the nations of the Middle East, especially the moderate Arab states, must open up their societies, and give the common people a voice.

By neglecting radical regimes, we set ourselves up for future conflicts. This is exactly what happened in Afghanistan after the Soviets left the country. The United States withdrew from the region, leaving Afghanistan in the hands of the Taliban.

As for Israel, the U.S. will have to continue to support it. It is the region's only functioning democracy, and it must survive. The U.S., however, needs to continue to push for peace between Israel and its Arab neighbors, and to find a solution to the Palestinian problem. Overcoming this hurdle will go a long way toward lasting peace in the region.

Militarily, as President George W. Bush has said, the U.S. must not distinguish between terrorists and the states that sponsor them. Countries that support terrorism must be stopped. Without state sponsorship, terrorist organizations will be dealt a severe blow. This is why the U.S. fought and destroyed the Taliban regime in Afghanistan in 2001 and 2002. The ultra-radical Taliban opened their country to Osama bin Laden and his terrorist network, allowing him the freedom to set up training camps and use the country as a base from which to lash out at the U.S. The individual terror networks must be dismantled by freezing their finances and hunting them down. Their leaders must be brought to justice and kept behind bars.

Stopping terrorism is a huge challenge, but already there are signs of hope. The world seems to be uniting behind American leadership. The September 11 attacks may have backfired on the terrorists. The destruction was so great that most countries of the world were outraged. They also realized that if something were not done, the horror could happen to them next.

Another point to remember is that the majority of Muslims do not agree with the actions of the radicals. If we can find a way to create hope and dignity for the people of the Middle East, we might just stamp out the roots of hatred and terror.

The Future?

Palestinian boys play with toy guns in the garbage-strewn Dheisheh refugee camp.

Major Mideast Terrorist Groups

al-Qaeda (the Base)

Goal: To set up a worldwide Islamic regime by destroying "non-Islamic" Western governments, especially the United States.

Location: Has operations in many countries worldwide.

Strength: May have thousands of members spread over the globe.

Overview: Al-Qaeda was formed by Saudi millionaire Osama bin Laden in the 1980s while fighting Soviet occupation forces in Afghanistan. The network gathered together thousands of Islamic fighters from all over the world to help oust the Soviets. They were also supported by the United States, which objected to the Soviet invasion of Afghanistan, although bin Laden was never directly aided by the U.S. government. Today al-Qaeda receives money from charities and donations from Muslim countries and organizations. It aids needy Muslims, but uses most of its money to fund terrorist operations around the world. Al-Qaeda is responsible for the bombing of U.S. embassies in Kenya and Tanzania, the bombing of the USS *Cole* while in port in Yemen, and the September 11 attacks on the World Trade Center and Pentagon.

HAMAS and Islamic Jihad

Goal: There are two groups within HAMAS, which stands for the Islamic Resistance Movement. The Islamic Jihad is usually considered a part of HAMAS. One of the HAMAS groups wants to create a Palestinian Islamic homeland and make a peace agreement with Israel. The other part of HAMAS seeks the total destruction of Israel.

Location: Syria, Israeli-controlled Palestinian areas, Israel, and Lebanon.

Strength: May include tens of thousands of members, although the actual number is unknown.

Overview: HAMAS started in 1987 as a more radical offshoot of the Palestinian branch of the Muslim Brotherhood. HAMAS gives aid, such as food and education, to Palestinian refugees. HAMAS has rebel cells that operate independently from the top leadership. Its goal is to use random violence, such as suicide bombings, to terrorize Israeli citizens. HAMAS is funded through wealthy individuals from other countries, as well as from Islamic states such as Iran.

Hezbollah

Goal: To create an Islamic state in Lebanon like the one in Iran, and to get rid of non-Islamic Western influences.

Location: Middle East, Europe, Latin America, and the U.S.

Strength: Membership in the thousands.

Overview: Hezbollah, whose name means "Party of God," got its start in 1983. It receives funds from charities and other donations, but is partly financed and supported by Iran. Hezbollah has a military section called Islamic Resistance. These terrorist guerrillas are known to be brutal and effective. They are trained and funded by Iran. They often use suicide bombers.

Timeline

1940-1945
Strategic bombing is used by both sides during World War II to inflict casualties among the enemy's civilian population. Millions are killed.

1944-1948
The Jewish Irgun armed resistance group uses terrorist tactics in the struggle to establish a Jewish homeland in Palestine. King David Hotel is bombed July 22, 1946.

1948-1949
First Arab-Israeli War. Thousands of Palestinians are forced into refugee camps.

1954-1962
Algerian militants use terrorism to effectively cause French colonial forces to withdraw and grant independence.

July 22, 1968
Palestinian terrorists hijack an Israeli jet, causing a tense 40-day standoff in Algeria.

September 5, 1972
Palestinian terrorists take Israeli athletes hostage during Munich Olympics. Negotiations fail, and 11 Israelis, five terrorists, and one German policeman die.

1979
The Shah of Iran is overthrown. The hard-line Islamic republic of Iran is born. On November 4, the U.S. embassy in Tehran is stormed. Approximately 70 Americans are held for 444 days.

1979-1989
Soviet Union invades and occupies Afghanistan. After 10 years, Muslim guerrillas force a Soviet withdrawal. Osama bin Laden's al-Qaeda terror network is born.

1990-1991
Persian Gulf War.

1998
Osama bin Laden calls for holy war against the United States, including the killing of civilians. U.S. embassies in Tanzania and Kenya are bombed.

2000
USS *Cole* is bombed while in port in Yemen.

September 11, 2001
Al-Qaeda terrorists crash two civilian jumbo jets into New York's World Trade Center, and a third into the Pentagon in Washington, D.C. The WTC is completely demolished; the Pentagon is extensively damaged. A fourth jet crashes in rural Pennsylvania after passengers revolt against the terrorists. In all, over 3,000 people are killed.

Where On The Web?

http://www.terrorism.com/index.shtml
Official site of the Terrorism Research Center. Dedicated to informing the public of the phenomena of terrorism and information warfare. The site features essays and thought pieces on current issues, as well as links to other terrorist documents, research, and resources.

http://travel.state.gov/travel_warnings.html
The U.S. Department of State issues public announcements and travel warnings on countries the U.S. government suspects of harboring terrorists.

http://www.fema.gov/old97/terror.html
The U.S. Federal Emergency Management Agency (FEMA) gives background information on terrorism.

http://www.odci.gov/cia/publications/factbook/
Facts and figures about every country, compiled by the United States Central Intelligence Agency (CIA).

http://www.defenselink.mil/pubs/almanac/
Defense Almanac, a site filled with facts and statistics about the United States Department of Defense.

Glossary

assassinate

To murder a person, especially someone politically important, like a president or king, by surprise attack. Assassins usually work for payment or because of a zealous belief. Terrorists often attempt to assassinate their political opponents.

civilian

A person who is not an active member of the armed forces, the police, or other organizations that have police power.

colony

A group of people who settle or reside in a distant land, but are under the political control of their native land. Colonies often fight for their freedom, such as the 13 British colonies that became the original United States of America.

democracy

A government made up of representatives who are freely elected by a majority of the citizens of a country. The United States is one of the oldest democracies in the world.

fatwa

An Islamic religious decree, or ruling, issued by a council of religious leaders. A *fatwa* is sometimes referred to as a death sentence imposed through such a decree. Osama bin Laden issued a *fatwa* in 1998, calling for Muslims to kill Americans.

guerrilla

A member of a small defensive force of soldiers. Guerrillas use surprise raids, often behind enemy lines, to disrupt an invading army or occupying force.

jihad

A holy war by Muslims against the enemies of Islam. Also the internal struggle of Muslims as they contemplate their faith, a spiritual striving for self-improvement.

martyr

Someone who would rather suffer or die instead of give up their faith or beliefs.

Pentagon

The huge, five-sided building near Washington, D.C., where the main offices of the U.S. Department of Defense are located.

smart bomb

A bomb or missile that navigates its way to a target, usually by following a laser beam "painted" on the target by a plane or special operations soldier on the ground. Smart bombs are usually very accurate, although they sometimes malfunction.

zealot

Someone who is a follower of a movement, often religious or political, to an unusual or extreme degree.

Zionism

The political and spiritual movement for supporting the Jewish state of Israel.

Index